SHE
WHO
DREAMS

JAMIE GALLANT

SHE
WHO
DREAMS

JAMIE GALLANT

Columbus, Ohio

She Who Dreams

Published by Gatekeeper Press
2167 Stringtown Rd, Suite 109
Columbus, OH 43123-2989
www.GatekeeperPress.com

ISBN (paperback): 9781662903755
eISBN: 9781662904554

CONTENTS

ACKNOWLEDGMENTS

For you mom, a strong, selfless and admirable superwoman. You're the one person who understands me. You're the one person who has given me everything. Sometimes I wonder how you did it, raising us three. Thank you for simply being you. I love you to the moon and back.

For my readers, you are incredible. Thank you for taking the time to read this book. More importantly, thank you for giving me a chance.

And for the people who love, dream, look up at the stars and wish, despite what they have gone through.

This is for you.

INTRODUCTION

People have walked out of my life without any explanations. They have walked out just when I was starting to trust again. I was the girl who was always there for people even if I was battling through my own problems. I used to overanalyze every situation, thinking I could have done more. I don't understand why people come and go, leaving you with the broken pieces. I was hurt, and that made it harder for me to trust people.

My parents' divorce scarred me in more ways than one. My dad wasn't really in my life at all. He didn't get to see me grow up. For years I was emotionally detached. I realized then, I shouldn't have to beg for relationships.

For a while I really thought there wasn't a happy ending for me. I dated a few people who were no good and I've dated ones that were sweet, but it never went anywhere. I found myself in many "situationships" and I abused myself mentally and emotionally, thinking I deserved it. It wasn't fair. I knew I wanted love, but I had to love myself first.

The one thing that got me through it all was writing. It was the only way I knew how to express my feelings. On occasion, I tend to keep things bottled up, but getting it out really challenged me for the better. Writing has become my therapy and my only means of survival.

Writing saved me.

This collection of poems has been written within the passage of time and were inspired by dreams that I could write novels about. Often times, I find myself going back to sleep trying to relive each dream. The people I talk about (no names of course) are the reason for all of this. Every word written here is purely inspired by family, exes, heartbreak and the twisting paths of love and loss.

I believe people are sent to us as guide to help us see things in a different light. Sometimes, the wrong ones walk out so better things can happen. Now, I find myself embracing the bad days, not something I could say before. I am super proud of this woman and if it wasn't for my pain, I'm not sure I would be relishing in this remarkable journey. It's time I heal my mind, body and soul and embrace the scars that truly make her beautiful.

I pray that my words resonate with you as you read how I turned my pain into ink. I hope my growth can help you to embrace yours. Growth is an uncomfortable process, but one that will always be worth it.

You owe it to yourself to dream,
love,
heal
and grow.

Bit by bit and piece by piece, I put myself back together again.
Even when others couldn't help me, I knew I had to help myself.
You would think I had a sign on my forehead that said,
"Please hurt me."
People gave my heart the runaround,
yet I still managed to hold on.

If that isn't strength, then I don't know what is.

THANKFUL FOR YOU

Thank you, mom, for all the hugs you gave.
Especially when I was sad or didn't behave.
You took on the role of both father and mother.
You are a rare breed, and there is no other.
There were days you said that it felt like hell.
Yet bravery and strength fit you all so well.
I loved story time and I remembered it the most.
I would say, "Again and again," because you were such a great host.
You treated story time like it was the final hour.
You taught me to never be a princess who needed
saving from a tower.
Instead you taught me to be a queen.
To lead by example, without causing a scene.
You instilled great values in me more than you know.
That's why I stayed out of trouble and kept it low.
I am always learning all there is to know from you.
Especially when it comes to what skirt goes with what shoe.
I have always been your stubborn little diva.
I wish I got the chance to meet Grandma Eva.
I love hearing stories from when you were my age.
You loved to dance like you belonged onstage.
Though I'm most thankful for your selflessness.
You are a powerful woman, so you were made for this.
I know it's not easy being a mother, especially as we get older.
But my job is to keep you warm as the world gets colder.
Radiate love that's all we can do.
Thank you again mama, I'm most thankful for you.

YOUR WINGS WERE READY,
BUT MY HEART WAS NOT

I never really wanted you to go, so many
things you should have known.
All the conversations I wanted to have, I always sense this nature
about you, so raw and unmasked.
You were a brilliant person something I always admired, but
God got jealous and took you in to get inspired.
You found your destiny towards the end of the light, so many
fond memories came into sight.
They say when you go your whole life flashes before your very
own eyes, but I don't believe anyone goes
away or really even dies.
I feel you with me every step of the way, I know you're with me
taking my hand day by day.
Growing up for me was kind of tough when you were not around,
but you told me you gave me space
to create my own kind of sound.
Very opinionated just like you, the apple doesn't fall
far from the tree, who would of knew.
They also say I am stubborn just like you,
but I tell them that couldn't possibly be true.
Again, that's my stubborn side speaking, I can't deny that I am
your daughter, I am always critiquing.

I miss you so much I have destroyed paths before me, so much to learn here but I know I will be free.

My brothers have this indent where their heart should be, I wish I could be a man for them like you once were to me.

Though I remember the special times the most, but the memories are so distant now I just want you close.

I have heart and it still beats, but what do I do when everybody weeps?

The tears start rolling down in remembrance of you, I wish everybody saw the kind of man you grew into.

Sure, you had your ways don't we all, but the saddest thing is I couldn't help you once you started to fall.

I wish I got to say I love you one last time, you're my forever friend and no one could replace you, not even this glass of wine.

I overindulge every now and then, I know I should stop because drinking was never your Zen.

As I get older, I'm starting to look like mama, but I talk like you and keep away from the drama.

God works in mysterious ways; you finally know now if he exists, a concept that kept you up for days.

I am no longer fixated on knowing all the answers, as long as our memories stay up like a room full of dancers.

For now, I will walk in the grace of my own tune, you'll never be forgotten, I'll be seeing you soon.

YOU'RE NEVER READY

Truth is whenever I hear bad news I completely shut down.
I get inside my own head and block out all the sound.
I don't take death well either and it changes my whole perspective.
I choose to show compassion because a little bit can be effective.
I never want anyone to endure sadness or go through pain.
Because in your moment of weakness you don't feel the same.
Love is humility but it can save lives.
Emotions are painful like you've been punctured
with thousands of knives.
You're never ready for something unexpected.
And bad news comes even if you're the least affected.
So, take this as you're never ready for what's to come.
That's why compassion and positivity is what I choose to become.

THE BEGINNING OF THE NEW BEGINNING OR THE BEGINNING OF THE END

Live in each moment for you never know it's your last.
Conquer your dreams before it becomes part of your past.
Life is too precious don't let it pass you by.
Everyone has a purpose, even you with that tear in your eye.
Don't ever lose hope because you're going through a tough time.
Because God answers prayers, and for that you'll be fine.
It's faith that brings you closer to the light.
Through the darkest times is when your strength propels you
back into sight.
Like a boat with a paddle it will never leave you astray.
Days like these aren't forever, you will soon find your way.
The worst is over now, and you can make it if you try.
Because it didn't happen overnight for those who are
now able to fly.

MIRROR, MIRROR

Mirror, mirror on the wall.
Will he catch me if I fall?
Will he keep me safe and warm?
Will he protect me and do no harm?
Am I the one for him?
Will the mood set right when lights are dim?
Am I his forever friend?
Will there be laughs that never end?
Am I rushing into this?
Am I blind sighted by his kiss?
Is there something else for me?
A shooting star that I cannot see?
Will my dreams be bright and vivid?
Or will I be the person who is unbending and rigid?
Though I have a lot to look forward to.
I need to take it easy, it's something I must do.
Because this is the life you have right now.
It's you in the mirror now take a bow.

LOVE NOT LOST

Everything for a reason.
People in love who lose feeling.
We adapt with every season.
And help friends who need healing.
We never give up, only weaken.
We have heart but that's too revealing.
We struggle and feel beaten.
Because this time last year you were sad but dealing.
Leaving you crooked and uneven.
Though there's hope for the broken and old heathen.
But love is not lost, just keep breathin'.

IGNORANCE IS BLISS

I carry this weight on me like it's all still fresh.
I think about you and I don't know what to do next.
I am so tired of loving and I'm so tired of hurting.
Sometimes the tears feel as if they're burning.
I wish I could help you save me from it all.
Because I can't get up from this great big fall.
We live in a world that moves so quickly and fast.
There's no telling if this relationship could last.
I have these emotions that I don't know how to channel.
I feel like everyone is judging me harshly but I'm the only
one at the panel.
I wish I could take you inside this brain of mine.
So I wouldn't have to lie and tell you everything is fine.
But you see, I have a lot of growing up to do.
I still have dreams that haven't come true.
I need to push myself to greater heights.
I have to stop blaming you and end these fights.
Though I am the reason for all this confusion.
Because these dreams are real and it's no illusion.
I believe it's hard for me since I am no good at moving on.
I wish these memories didn't replay like the radio
does with a song.
Is this what happens when you have loved and lost?
I am starting to wonder if this is the cost.
I have dealt with so many things in my twenty-five years of living.

Yet I still can't grasp the simple act of forgiving.
I must forgive so I can free myself.
The story has finished now put it back on the shelf.
I'm slowly losing faith that I can't recover from this.
So, in the theme of my life, ignorance is bliss.

BEGIN AGAIN

It's crazy to think that I was in a different place last year.
I was begging for the things that are now so close and dear.
I always used to say, "Time heals all."
If you saw me then I was barely able to crawl.
I guess life is strange like that.
It's the not knowing or where you'll be at.
I must talk myself into these kinds of states.
Because the pressure weighs heavy, like box crates.
Do you ever just stop and think?
What if your life was different in just one blink?
Would you keep your eyes wide open in fear that you're
changing your destiny?
Or will you close them shut in hopes that it
will change eventually?
You can keep trying until you get it right.
Because you can't give up without one last fight.
In the scene of the movie where men encounter bloodshed.
They still give it their all without knowing what's ahead.
Your life is just like the movies, despite what's real.
Because even the best of us have what we call "the Achilles' heel."
I know it's not easy and difficult at best.
But living an honest life is truly the test.
You have everything you need right inside of you.
There's always tomorrow where you will be
presented with something new.

Life is a beautiful mystery.
But it's up to you to make history.
There is so much hope and wonder.
But it stays still if you sit and ponder.
And if you must take a break every now and then.
Just remember to pick back up and begin again.

YOU WERE NEVER MINE

You left me in the dirt with a broken heart.
For all the things you've done, I don't know where to start.
I really thought you were the one for me.
But you and I are just an old memory.
I couldn't help but fall for you.
But when you were down, I didn't know what to do.
I know she was the one that got away.
But for me being in denial, it just felt better that way.
You used to say I was perfect and deserved better.
But you kept me warm like an old comfy sweater.
I never thought you would leave like you did.
You left without warning like you fell off the grid.
I couldn't save you from all the pain you endured.
Because a broken heart can only be mended, but never cured.
Though I have been there at your lowest.
Yet I was the one moving the slowest.
I couldn't get away from you if my life depended on it.
I just wish you and I were a perfect fit.
But you plagued my heart from the moment we met.
You robbed me of my love and now I'm stuck with debt.
But I am hopeful for a love that's greater than me.
And once I do, I will finally be set free.
Even though you were probably my favorite chapter.
I wasn't the love you were seeking after.
Good luck or break a leg as they say.
Because you really never cared anyway.

IN MY DREAMS

You were in my dreams last night.
You spoke words of fright.
You told me I'm doing it all wrong.
You were going off on this tangent that sounded like a song.
I had nothing to say so I walked away.
Hoping you would get the point and see things my way.
I couldn't believe that it was you that I saw.
Even here I can't escape you it may well be my tragic flaw.
Do I harbor something inside that needs some reinforcement?
Is this dream trying to tell me something important?
Do I need to strengthen the relationship I have with myself?
Am I repressing a side of me that is not my true authentic self?
Am I in need of that full emotional closure?
Am I realizing that life is too short and I'm getting older?
I guess our soul agreements with a few people are eternal.
Like how your soul can decode life like it knows everything written in your journal.
I am my own self-fulfilling prophecy.
I need to stop over thinking and let the course flow naturally.
Even though I have improved at the whole "not over thinking."
It just feels like I misplaced my energy and now I'm sinking.
Have I blown it and disrupted my fate?
Have I finally arrived to find out I'm late?
I know what I need to do, and I have to stop neglecting.
And there's no better way to start than by reflecting.

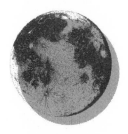

UNFINISHED BUSINESS

You hit me up to reminisce over the past.
Could have guessed this conversation would end so fast.
You claim you're happy and doing alright.
But I wasn't the one dreaming of me last night.
I forgot all about you and here you are again.
I used to wonder what we could have been.
Truth is we always vibrated on the same frequency.
Except our true feelings were cloaked in secrecy.
You acted like you wanted me.
But you and I were never a guarantee.
We are more alike than you can imagine.
But your follow through comes with no action.
Sometimes I try to guess your type.
But the suspense no longer keeps me up at night.
We got caught up in a very bad habit.
Your heart would be mine if you only let me grab it.
Your mixed signals made me question how I should feel.
Our relationship didn't exactly feel so real.
You always kept me in the dark.
I'm not even sure you felt a spark.
I know I wasn't the only one you claimed to miss.
You kept me at bay, what a major diss.
But I want to say thank you for paving the way for my growth.
I promised myself and took an oath.
That the next time you invite me to this "dance."

I will no longer entertain your ego like you still hold a chance.
Though there's something worth mentioning.
Your sweet embrace is hypnotizing and beckoning.
But let's face the facts.
We will always be unfinished business, show's over, no more acts.

FREE FALL

He does not recognize himself anymore.
He's praying there is a God above to save him from
this internal war.
He's on the bathroom floor begging please.
His negative thoughts strike like a gruesome disease.
He's fighting a battle no one knows about.
Happiness dies every periodical drought.
He wonders if there is something out there for him.
His eyes never looked so lifeless and dim.
He keeps thinking about the one that got away.
Skies never looked so gloomy and grey.
Because she was his light when he couldn't see.
Even when they fought and couldn't agree.
He'd rather fight with her than not have her at all.
Because you don't figure out love, you free fall.

EMERALD SKY

Meet me under the emerald sky.
Where the children of the forest lie.
I talk to the trees and hear them whisper.
They say, "Tell her you love her and kiss her."
Her eyes shine brighter than all of the stars.
She makes me forget all of my scars.
I walk down the path that leads to nowhere.
I listen to the winds, so I know I'm almost there.
Because love never danced so finely at night.
Suddenly the darkness felt so light.
Underneath the emerald sky.
Our love untouched, will never die.

DEPART AND DON'T LOOK BACK

I search for your name in my phone and you are not there.
But when I look around me, I see you everywhere.
I draw this line but there is no trace of you.
Sometimes you need to be in another's arm to know you grew.
The clutter of one relationship became a toxic wasteland.
It wasn't long before I started sinking deep, like quicksand.
Sometimes the wrong ones end up teaching us the most.
Now I look at love like I have seen a ghost.
"But don't be afraid," is what they say,
"Nothing lasts forever it's just a bad day."
I need to mend the fragments that have broken off.
Love is vulnerable so it's okay to be soft.
I have witnessed dark times and ecstasy highs.
You are allowed to walk away without saying your goodbyes.
Departure looks a lot like growth.
Thinking about it now I must have done both.
Closing an old chapter gives you a sense of cleanliness.
But regret gives you a feeling of emptiness.
Just look how far you have come.
Now keep moving forward, your story has just begun.

RECYCLED HEART

You've been used and lied to over and over again.
I kept you close because you were my only friend.
Even when you were vulnerable and naive.
You kept pumping and let me grieve.
Oh, recycled heart.
You always knew right from the start.
Although you managed to keep me alive.
Those tormented days killed me inside.
When I couldn't find the strength or the courage.
You still managed to pump and flourish.
Oh, recycled heart.
You're actually brave and exceedingly smart.
You were misunderstood for so long.
But only to those who couldn't sing along.

LOVE IS AROUND THE CORNER

When you know it's no good for you, but you don't care.
Because a life with adventure is just your flare.
You like where he takes you and the vision he sees.
The temperature is brewing to 100 degrees.
I know it's not simple, but darling, nothing is.
Sooner or later he will give it a shot and you'll be his.
Love is the way and love is the answer.
I've twirled around love before; I, the dancer.
So, I know when I'm coming on to something special.
You can give it your all but first be gentle.
Sometimes emotions run deep, and it gets harder
to push through.
Just look at what love made you do.
Don't ever compromise your feelings and mask them away.
Because this romance could be yours someday.
Live in the present because it takes you so far.
Love is around the corner, it's actually what you are.

MISFIRE

For all the times I cried I was only addressing my feelings.
For all the times I made them my own was only the
effort of my healings.
I never knew how strong emotions could be.
I really did try to be this person that wasn't me.
I got rid of people who hindered my growth and who were toxic.
I had to walk away before it became a conflict.
The weight feels so much lighter now.
I knew I could walk away, and betrayal showed me how.
Now I can talk about the good memories without feeling somber.
Because those friends of mine weren't really friends
I could honor.
I think about life now and try to fit them in the equation.
But I wouldn't have changed one thing, not even through persuasion.
I am happy I'm around good energy and I am around people
who believe in me.
Because what I called a friendship was actually a misfire,
a sad tragedy.

YOU

Let's bring it back to the day you noticed me.
You were everything I wanted – just how a man should be.
You had class and style something I was instantly attracted to.
You introduced yourself to me and I was glad it was you.
You had this spirit I easily recognized.
You couldn't dance well but your touch had me paralyzed.
You had big brown eyes and light brown hair.
We looked cute together I thought, a perfect pair.
But you lived far, and we only talked about dreams.
And if you wanted to, I would move tomorrow as
crazy as that seems.
I think you were afraid of being let down.
Because there you stayed, put back in your hometown.
But I never asked you to move or change up your life.
Now I must begin this long journey without you no
matter the strife.
But I hope you find somebody who chooses you every day.
Because fate had other plans and life just got in the way.
I was finishing up school and you were starting your new career.
All I wanted to do was see you or at least have you near.
But I'm happy knowing you're where you're supposed to be.
But I keep reminiscing the day we met when you were into me.

FORBIDDEN FRUIT

I have this feeling that you may be into me.
But my love is pricey and isn't for free.
I love the way you remember all of my favorite things.
But I must warn you I am not really into flings.
I am aware that she's been there for a while.
But I don't judge it's not like you're here on trial.
But can I let you in on a little secret too?
For the moment we met, something rang true.
I don't know what it was perhaps it was the way you listened.
And maybe for one second the thought of you glistened.
But I don't want to pry or get in the way.
Because you can't make someone yours if they're not
willing to stay.
I know you're settling because that's what we do.
And maybe my perception on love is a little blue.
But what do I know only you know the truth.
I'm only reacting and making sense of my youth.
But you really need to help me out.
I can't make sense of this or what you're even about.
I can't entertain you forever.
And as the saying goes, "Reason deceives us often,
conscience never."
And maybe what we have here is innocent.
And maybe the thought of me is so far and distant.
I guess I'll never know how you feel.
But when it comes to companionship, I'm the real deal.

PERMANENT GRIEF

I hope you're proud of me and all that I have accomplished.
You were worried in the beginning, but I finished school
just like I promised.
We didn't have the relationship I always craved.
But I have a man now who is gold and somehow, I feel saved.
Cheers to the nights I couldn't sleep.
I channeled that into writing where I got deep.
In a way writing has become my therapy.
This is when I realized with blinding clarity.
I miss you more than ever, I'm just sad we didn't have more time.
And every now and then I look around for a sign.
When the birds flock together, and the winds get stronger.
I feel your presence lurking and my heart grows fonder.
My feelings are my own and no one gets to decide that for me.
Love is priceless so that makes it free.
I don't care what they think they know because I dealt with pain
much differently.
If the tables were turned, I am sure they would loathe all negativity.
I never thought a passing could unveil someone's true color.
And with life these days we are all still trying to recover.
You never know how valuable a life is until it's no longer there.
But I'll be damned if I see another person shame me into silence
or say I didn't care.
My childhood wasn't exactly something I remember being easy.
But I never made excuses I just carried on when days

weren't so breezy.
Let's all take a step back and be thankful for just being alive.
And take every set back or difficulty as a moment to thrive.
I may not be perfect, but neither are they.
And maybe I'll use their pity to my disposal someday.

OLD MEMORY

I know what you're doing, and it works every time.
Because when you call, I almost forget I am not fine.
I don't even remember why we parted.
But I remember how we met and how it started.
You were patiently waiting for your interview.
And when you looked up instantly, you knew.
You did a double take to make sure your eyes did
not deceive you.
And when I walked closer, I could tell you had this feeling too.
Our eyes locked and suddenly we remembered.
That this wasn't the first time we've met; we've known
each other forever.
What brought us here we may never know.
Because at some point we stopped elevating; we couldn't grow.
You brought out my demons, but you tamed them as well.
I'm so sorry but now you're just a story I can tell.
Sadly, I realized what you were to me.
But I refused to admit it; I refused to see.
You were needed in my life but not to stay.
Now you're just an old memory I can share with my kids someday.

LAST LOVE LAST FOREVER

You told me that our love would be forever.
But I can't decide for you, it's either now or never.
Unfortunately, you chose to turn your back on us.
Now once again my heart must adjust.
Even when you were down and feeling blue.
You told me, "My mind, body and soul were waiting for you."
You saw that I held an extraordinary gift.
And just like that you felt a subtle shift.
You told me I was something special but in the cosmic sense.
And anyone before me was fake, a false pretense.
You never understood why I humbled myself or tried
to hide away.
You said a beauty like mine isn't something you come
across every day.
Sometimes it works out in the end and sometimes it doesn't.
As far as saying sorry I wouldn't say it if I wasn't.
We must respect that the universe knew what it was doing when
it began and when it ended.
And with energy now I am careful how I spend it.
Learn to trust the natural order of things.
And just when you least expect it, you'll be grateful for
what it brings.
Last love last forever.
There must be a reason we are no longer together.

SEA FULL OF DREAMS

I don't find myself fighting against it anymore.
I'm just slowly sweeping on the bottom of the ocean floor.
The water flows steady when I'm all alone.
But tides get heavy when I can't see home.
Nobody here for me, nobody cares.
I seek for answers; I wish for prayers.
In a sea full of dreams, I'm misunderstood.
But darkness subsides as it always should.
Sometimes I weep but my tears fade into the sea.
Why can't anyone see but me?
I often struggle to find the real ones.
When it comes to friends it's like I'm watching reruns.
Until you understand that it's you in the reflection.
You begin to learn your sense of direction.
Because when it comes to others, I often hit a wall.
Like a tide you have the rise and the fall.
I don't find myself fighting against it anymore.
I'm just slowly sweeping on the bottom of the ocean floor.
In a sea full of dreams, you'll find yourself alone.
Because your vision is yours, no one else's but your own.
You can go to great lengths if you just keep swimming.
Even when people try to prevent you from winning.
But in a sea full of dreams...
Anything is possible, as crazy as that seems.

STAY TRUE TO YOU

Four years ago, I was unraveling the essence of my nature.
I knew Jamie was shedding skin and I couldn't keep her.
I was destined for something greater than me.
I knew she was growing but to what degree?
I wasn't prepared for what was about to come.
But she gave me hope when I was numb.
Even though I saw some things I wish I didn't see.
I realize it wouldn't have brought the person I was meant to be.
I am forever thankful for the weight that turned into pressure.
Now I look at failing as a refresher.
Because it's better to keep trying and see yourself fail.
You can't survive the storm if you're afraid to sail.
I've grown so much already, and I am happy I am me.
Because I worked so hard for her and I am right where
I'm supposed to be.
Even though I may have more learning to do.
The biggest thing I've learned so far is the importance
of being true to you.

UNDERTOW

Meet me in the undertow.
Where most are afraid to go.
I can show you things that may startle you.
Because it's foreign and something new.
Just close your eyes and visualize.
The world is deceived, don't believe its lies.
We can find hope here; love will be our guide.
In the undertow is where we will hide.
You are a beautiful cosmic energy.
Don't ever try to compromise to something you'll never be.
Together our love will grow.
In the undertow is where we'll go.

A NEW KIND OF LOVE

I will follow to wherever this takes me.
Maybe you can be mine, my safety.
And maybe you can call this crazy.
But everyone before you left me hazy.
I really want to explore you, the parts that are unknown.
Just know with me you'll never be alone.
You are special I just want you to know.
And no matter what this is, I will follow.
There is something about your eyes when I speak.
There is something about your quirky walk that makes me weak.
I know we're playing with fire.
But your touch is the one I desire.
I can't help but think about you.
Suddenly the thought makes me feel brand new.
I can be yours if only you tried.
But you need to reveal your feelings instead of
keeping them inside.
Just take my hand and watch the storm fade away.
Because a new kind of love is here on display.

GLOW IN THE DARK

Please pick my brain apart.
Find out my dreams and get to know my heart.
See my light as well as the dark.
Let's torch this union, this incredible spark.
I am no longer afraid when I am with you.
Please tell me you feel this too.
Can I take you down that glistening road?
Where dreams were once crushed, but still rivers flowed?
Most nights I lay awake with the attempt to recover.
But you saw me for me, all the parts you were willing to discover.
You helped me to see my true potential.
You are my biggest fan and so influential.
You are my sunrise when I am feeling low.
Your presence radiates a warm glow.
You are the cloak that keeps me warm.
And when my clouds are grey, you take away the storm.
I was miserable before I met you.
Now I look at love with an incredible view.

A FATHER'S SACRIFICE

What if he lost everything just so you could be saved?
What if the love you end up with helps you remember
what was paved?
And maybe you let me hate you instead.
Because the truth was too hurtful, so it was better left unsaid.
I guess I realize that now and I'm sorry I didn't see.
I hate that I was so blind and let you do this to me.
I guess you did this to keep me from hurting others.
Because when you saw the world black and white, I saw colors.
But you looked fear in the eyes, and you understood the sacrifice.
Even if it costed you everything you knew, it wasn't a fair price.
My life was too precious, and you wanted me to live.
Even for the times I couldn't stand you and when I couldn't forgive.
But truth is you can't tear people down to make yourself feel better.
And maybe I still try to understand it like a secret code in an
encrypted letter.
But maybe what you did was actually what I needed after all.
Because the truth smacks you hard and you couldn't
bear to see me fall.
And even though courage and strength fit me.
Strong is not what you wanted me to be.
I can see that now and choices are never easy to make.
Because we are only responsible for how we give
and how we take.
I'm so sorry if this all caused me to stand still and be uncertain.

But truth is I never wanted you to carry this burden.
You were only doing your best because you too have
endured so much pain.
The thoughts of you creep harder now, but the
memories of you remain.

BAD AT LOVE

I'm so bad at love and I think I know why.
Cause if they ask how I feel I would rather lie.
It's like my thoughts make sense but my words do not.
So, I'd rather say a little than a lot.
I find it extremely hard to open up and express how I feel.
I feel like I am always trying to hide cause I'm afraid
what I might reveal.
I wonder if anyone else ever feels this way.
Because when it comes to my feelings it's hard to say.
I felt like the moment we cut ties I lost my direction.
Now I'm feeling nothing these days catches my attention.
I'm so used to the feeling of disappointment.
And love just called I'm late to my appointment.
He was an outsider just like me.
But now I'm struggling for the answer I cannot see.
Your heart is always one step ahead.
Because you can't always listen to the thoughts in your head.
Because if you look inward you will see what I mean.
You represent all things unknown and unseen.
I guess you are by far my biggest fear.
Because even when I try, I can't keep you near.
Somehow, we keep finding our way back to one another.
But I only know how to make you my part time lover.
I apologize a million times for I am no good at love.
And hopefully this fear will be something I grow out of.

CLOUDS

Sometimes I feel like I constantly have a cloud over my head.
Most days I feel tired and I just want to go to bed.
I can't shake this cloud that hangs over me.
I feel like darkness is where I'm supposed to be.
Does it ever get easier or do we just deal?
Why do I hurt so much why do I feel?
I'm so sick of feeling like I don't belong.
We only have one life but why does it feel so wrong.
Pessimism has taken a toll over me.
Because I've been holding in this pain when I should set it free.
I wasn't always like this as a child.
My imagination used to run free and wild.
I had so much exploration on my mind.
Now I keep wondering if I'm wasting my time.
I am so tired of feeling broken where sadness turns into hate.
I am starting to think these bad days have become my fate.
It's not like anyone calls anymore.
But then again, it's not like they did before.
Few have come forth for I was better off alone.
I try to fight this cloud but it's hard when that's all
that was shown.
And even though the clouds hang over me.
I am learning to let go and let things unravel naturally.
For your strength overpowers your darkness.
Now let this poem be sheer witness.

That despite what you are going through.
This poem can speak to you.
And if you are reading this.
Then I know you have surpassed your demons you
no longer miss.

YOU LIVE YOU LEARN

Last night I had a dream that I was chasing you
down cross country.
I felt like I had no choice and my mood was changed abruptly.
We had a plan to meet somewhere exclusive so you
wouldn't get caught.
But the entire time I was more scared about the
feelings I had brought.
I thought I was over you but here you are again having
me chase after you.
Even knowing all the obstacles in between all you
had to do was ask me to.
Waking up I have better clarity knowing that
relationship was completely one-sided.
But when we are young sometimes our actions
are foolishly misguided.
I still chased after you even knowing all the baggage
that came with you.
But it never occurred to you what I was willing to go through.
Sometimes in life we'd rather go through pain if that
meant we got the one in the end.
But there you were running with no real intentions
and refusing to bend.
You were so good at giving me just enough so I wouldn't go.
But that's not what I needed in order to grow.
Now that I'm older I can say this truthfully.
The pain you caused granted me something better,
a learning opportunity.

TRUTH IS

Truth is we all just want someone to hold onto;
someone we can trust.
Someone we can say forever to and know there is no distrust.
But truth is we just want someone there, so we
know someone cares.
The person you look for when you are scared because with
them there are no nightmares.
And someone to save us from the loneliness that
creeps late at night.
Someone who never let's go and holds on so tight.
We just need our person who can show us the movement.
They'll never steer you wrong because together you
see better improvement.
Truth is, love is powerful when it's unified.
I have so much love I can feel it inside.
I won't let who I was stop me from who I'm becoming.
And if love is all I have then I will keep on loving.
I truly have so much love to give.
A kind of love you would want to relive.
I see that this may be asking for a lot.
But if this journey brings me closer to love then
I will give it a shot.

LOST SOUL

I feel so lost and I don't know what to do.
When it comes to my dreams, I'm just trying to see it through.
I want to change the world and make things happen.
I remember the little girl with a paint brush back then.
She believed she could color the world with just
a little bit of paint.
But most days are looking pale, and the memory of her is faint.
I know I have a purpose and it's much bigger than these jobs.
These premonitions are real because my head hurts; it throbs.
I have this vision, but it feels so far.
I look into the distance and see the brightest star.
The light will lead you home, do you see it shine?
Because your light glows bright, it's shining all the time.
Be so immersed in your truth because it's all you can do.
Your path doesn't have to make sense to anyone but you.
And if you find the courage to start all over again.
Then I applaud you on your bravery because it suits you, my friend.
Just keep getting back up because life is much more than this.
Don't worry about the setback, it's just another thing you can dismiss.
I must be patient that the universe has something in store for me.
Because I believe I am on the path to my true destiny.

SILENCE

The sun came down and there I was trapped in my loneliness.
You were lying next to me, but I was full of emptiness.
I want to give you love but I can't even smile.
And most days I try, but I can't go the mile.
I'm not even sure how to snap out of this feeling.
I'm praying a lot lately; I'm longing for a healing.
I'm just searching for something meaningful.
So I can congregate a feeling that's truly incredible.
I'm searching for a happy place where I can shelter my thoughts.
But happiness is like a puzzle and I'm trying to connect the dots.
My mental state has been low and it's troubling for me.
Too many and too often people tell me to be carefree.
Because depression is silent and doesn't make a sound.
When a person is hurting, they try to keep no one around.
Sometimes we undermine a person's illness.
And as a result, we act like it's none of our business.
Lending a hand to a person in need is all it takes.
For them waking up is a chore and the world is full of heartbreaks.
The best thing we can do for each other is be there.
Because we never know when someone is hurting so it's time to
be more aware.
Mental health starts and ends with action.
So, remember this: Love will be the recipe and love
will be the distraction.

MOVING ON

It's not what you said it's how you said it.
Whenever I let you in you make me regret it.
Your definition of love is equivalent to a loose cannon.
You make it hard for me to walk in the shoes I stand in.
You have so much to give but nothing at all.
Your weight is enough for me to fall.
And now the nights feel like an eternity.
With your loss of control, I struggled with adversity.
It's not what you did it's how you did it.
And whatever this is, I no longer want part of it.

IT'S A TWIN THING

When you hurt, I am bruised.
When you get lost, I am confused.
When you are sad, I am too.
If you ever need a hand, I am here for you.
If you need a heart, I can give you mine.
If you need forever all I got is time.
You're God's greatest gift to me.
Even when we argue and can't agree.
I want to help, please tell me what to do.
Cause you fight off love like it wasn't meant for you.
But there's nothing I wouldn't do.
Because I am not me if there isn't two.

MEMORY OF YOU

The memory of you lives forever in my heart.
You had many talents, but your legacy spoke in your art.
You drew better than anyone I knew.
And the words you spoke pierced right through.
I bet you didn't even notice how special you really were.
So I refuse to let the memory of you become a blur.
The unhappier I am the more I can't forget you.
Because sad people keep reliving the past, it's what we do.
But it's the only way to keep the memory of you alive.
Even if this pain kills me inside.
I know this sounds abnormal, but it makes sense to me.
I bet this isn't the person you expected me to be.
I know I shouldn't feel so sad after all this time.
But the day you left I swore I'd never be fine.
Truth is I'd do anything to have you back.
Because life these days are falling off track.

CHASING HAPPINESS

I'm chasing after the time when I was young.
I'm breathing in air; I'm basking in the sun.
I'm falling in leaves; I'm playing with dirt.
I'm climbing the slides; my knees are hurt.
I miss my eight year old self always adventuring out.
With not a care in world, not a single doubt.
She keeps calling but I'm afraid to answer.
I wish I could stop this fear from spreading like cancer.
I guess most could say I was quiet as a child.
I had my moments and acted out every once in a while.
But I remember one thing that never really left my brain.
I remember asking myself, "Who am I and why do I have a name?"
How is it that I'm talking to myself and how am I alive?
And why are so many so talented but lack the drive?
I guess this poem can sum up my life in a nutshell.
Sometimes I question my own thoughts and think "What the hell."
Because fear is dangerous and only ignites when you light it.
I'm just glad I made it this far and didn't quit.
Now I know what my parents must of went through.
Because fear strikes down hard and doesn't warn you.
I'm chasing happiness and it's a long-winded run.
As a child I thought adulting would be so much fun.
Although I try to make the best of every situation.
I'm always looking for a meaning, some would call it desperation.
So, keep reminding yourself that you will never be truly satisfied.

And keep your loved ones close by your side.
And I think most would agree that we all have confessions.
One being that love will bring us joy, not our possessions.
So, realize that happiness doesn't have to go away.
Because happiness is a journey you choose every day.

POLITIK

When I didn't understand you, I still tried to find the light.
Even if your battles weren't my battles to fight.
Even when you stood your ground and had to be right.
I tried to see it in your eyes even if you lost sight.
I never asked much from you nor should I feel bad if I did.
You make it seem like it's a crime to want to give.
I want to believe that you would be there for me in the end.
I want to believe you wouldn't abandon me if I didn't have a friend.
I know you've built up walls to protect your fears.
But it's unfair when you don't acknowledge my face full of tears.
But I can't confide in the same place that left
me emotionally homeless.
Lately I rather be comforted by this illusion of wholeness.
But I would never treat you the way you did to me.
You say I am a burden but I had no reason to be.
I never expected anything from you and that's what pains me inside.
You think you're the only person with feelings to hide.
But you broke what took me forever to rebuild.
Does it hurt you knowing your politic was the only
thing you've instilled?
I feel worse than I ever did before.
You had no problem with showing me the door.
But I am moving on and I am getting strong.
The difference between you and I is you rather hate than be wrong.
And here I am trying to be what you couldn't be for me.
You can think all you want but I am not the enemy.

HOPELESS DREAM

You let me give your stuff back and I was broken hearted.
You told me the reason was her and that's why we parted.
You said she was the one and you're sorry you didn't realize.
But I can see it written on your face and I can see it in your eyes.
You don't love her because she doesn't challenge you
the way I do.
You really have no idea what I could do for you.
She can give you the sea, but I can give you the ocean.
But you're hard at love and you give off no emotion.
Stop being so stubborn and tell me you want me.
And if it isn't me then I'll leave you be.
I never understood why we couldn't be together.
Now seasons come and go, and I can't even measure.
You give me an equation for I am no good at math.
Bring on the storm so I can give you a better aftermath.
This isn't love this is just a catastrophe.
I can bring you close but I can't make you see.
Love isn't as easy as they make it seem.
So, you and I are nothing but a hopeless dream.

SOUL SEARCH

I am sorry that it took me so long.
I had to figure out what was going on.
I never meant to do you wrong.
And I'm sorry if this sounds like a sappy song.
My aura was as bright as the golden sun.
And I swear I used to be so much fun.
Now I'm looking for a sign so I can run.
And even when we weren't done.
I walked too soon and kept it shut.
Patching my pain like there was no cut.
I swear I feel like I'm the chosen one.
Emotions got the best of me, they really won.
And no, I'm not misunderstood.
People are behaving as they should.
I really am sorry for what I put you through.
I'm not even sure what to do.
I'm trying to figure out my next big move.
I'm searching for ways so I can improve.
Because if I don't take ahold of this now.
I will be resenting you somehow.
I really need to soul search a bit.
And just maybe you and I can be a perfect fit.

LOVER'S DEN

Merciful greens so full of life.
The grass grows tall to the perfect height.
Not a cloud in the sky, it is clear as day.
Lover's Den has become my favorite hideaway.
I don't know why I was even afraid.
Right beside me is the most perfect cascade.
First my toes take a dip and then I splash my face.
All this while I was aching for such a sweet embrace.
I look over to my right and the birds are flocking together.
The air feels so nice, I couldn't picture better weather.
I take a sit on the crystallized rock and I face my
head towards the sun.
Mr. Sun is putting on a show; I can tell he's having fun.
I can sit here all day long and never grow tired.
Suddenly I feel warm and greatly inspired.
But truth is it doesn't exist I only see it in my dreams.
Now reality seems estranged, it isn't as it seems.
For now, I will close my eyes and go back to sleep.
So Lover's Den is a memory I can keep.

EMOTIONAL ANCHOR

She counts on no one to be her emotional anchor.
At the highest tower with no one to save her.
Now she'd rather go through pain alone.
Weary of negativity, her solitude speaks for its own.
Because the fear of judgment means vulnerability.
And when it comes to her feelings it's no urgency.
She is used to others putting themselves first.
She never knew friendships could hurt the most.
Now she sees the truth for what it really is.
There's nothing wrong with wanting to love and wanting to live.
So cautious she remains with eyes wide open.
Guilt is such a wasted emotion.
Don't ever feel guilty for the gift of feeling.
Their toxicity shouldn't be your dealing.
But ironically, she was made for this.
Even when she rarely experiences days of bliss.
She counts on no one to be her emotional anchor.
Then they wonder what went wrong with her.

CONFESSIONS OF A COMPLEX MIND

Do you ever lie awake at night and think about tomorrow?
Do you feel like the hours go fast and the days are full of sorrow?
Do you ever get curious and check the weather in other countries?
Imagining yourself under the sun and next to tall palm trees?
Or touring around Turkey but then again that's too far.
Sometimes I think my mind gets kind of bizarre.
Do you make a checklist and hope to have it done by the
end of the year?
But when you realize you checked off nothing do you
shrivel up with fear?
Is it too soon to say I failed at life?
Can I break free from these thoughts that keep me up at night?
Traveling is something I wish I could do all the time.
I guess these are the confessions of a complex mind.
My spirit no longer wants to be in shadow.
There are so many places I'm willing to go.
But this complex mind will tell me it's impossible and unrealistic.
And what's worse is being somewhere that stops you
from being artistic.
Have we lost ourselves in these jobs and have we become blind?
I guess these are the confessions of a complex mind.
Help me get there I know you want it too.
So you can tell me I'm not the only one who thinks the way I do.

NEW ME

I'm feeling like nothing can stop me.
I'm right where I'm supposed be.
I guess this is what solitude feels like.
I've been working for hours it's going to be a long night.
I'm going to finally enjoy this ride.
I'm learning to accept the thoughts lying inside.
I have never been easy on myself, this I know.
I'm just trying to live and create as I go.
I'm never better; I'm lighter than air.
I'm clearing space for my self-care.
This is the greatest high; I'm feeling unstoppable.
I'm no longer hard on myself and this feeling is incredible.
I'm at the phase of true self-acceptance and I'm letting things be.
I am throwing away the worries before they consume me.
I love myself and I love this new me.
In case you weren't aware self-acceptance is free.

A KIND OF LIFE

What kind of life do I want this to be?
It would be a life that was meant for me.
I would have super powers and fly to somewhere new.
Travel the world so I know what I read is true.
I would fall in love with being an outsider.
Seeing the world would expand my mind wider.
I would fall in love with the culture and the trends
that take place.
I would wear the wool and cotton with such honor and grace.
I would love the kind of life that sees perspective.
Waking up each day with a fond introspective.
I would live a life that doesn't judge harshly.
But I would judge because I'm only human, just not constantly.
My life is a life I get to call my own.
As long as I don't forget the place I call home.
I would live a life full of love and laughter.
I would want a life where every day is my happily ever after.
What kind of life do I want this to be?
A life where I'm appreciative knowing nothing comes for free.

YOU AND ME

I don't know why the sky is blue or why the grass is green.
I don't understand why people never say what they truly mean.
Nothing makes sense except for you and me.
I don't know why we hide like we are not free.
Or why we don't know who we want to be.
Nothing makes sense except for you and me.
I don't know why we are not together or why she still
occupies your time.
I don't know why love is so hard to find.
Nothing makes sense except for you and me.
You are everything I want, and I hope you want this too.
I'd face my fears if I knew it brought me to you.
I am no good at ignoring my feelings.
I am sorry if I'm involving you in these dealings.
Because nothing makes sense except for you and me.

BLEAK MIDWINTER

In the bleak midwinter you lost your battle for survival.
Your fate rested solely in the hands of your rival.
Here comes the rain again as truths unfold.
Life is for the living who do what they're told.
The moment you left the earth shifted.
You're finally free and your chains are lifted.
And life after you is just borrowed time.
Not having you here makes it harder to climb.
The bleak midwinter awaited your arrival.
Our wounded spirits ache for spiritual revival.

FULL MOON

Tonight is a full moon.
I looked up in honor of you.
Fate has brought us together.
On account of the night's clear weather.
My eyes shine like the stars that twinkle and gleam.
You're a fantasy; you feel like a dream.
If tonight is all I have then I don't want to look down.
Because the sky is illuminated by thoughts of you now.
The grass shimmers by the moon's light.
If your love is on the moon, I would schedule my next flight.
The earth would get jealous by this moon's phase.
I can see my future in your eyes; I'm caught in a daze.
You make me whole without knowing that you do.
Suddenly I'm captivated by the moon's perception of you.
Tonight is a full moon and it's the final hour.
I am forever consumed by the moon's infinite power.
If you can see it now you would be changed forever.
I never want to leave nightfall, not now not ever.

THIS ISN'T THE END

I've said it once and I will say it again.
There doesn't have to be an end.
Cars keep moving and time doesn't stand still.
But you must stay strong when it's going downhill.
People will shock you in more ways than one.
When you accept your truth just know the healing has begun.
Don't ever compromise yourself to fit into their story.
You don't have to be sorry for your path to glory.
As long as you don't make excuses for yourself or others.
You can paint a beautiful picture but soon you'll use
up all of the colors.
Don't allow this time to open up old wounds.
May your heart be soft and lay among the delicate blooms.
You don't have to do anything that you don't want to do.
You are allowed to walk away from something that
no longer serves you.
And remember that being yourself doesn't have to
mean you're sorry.
The growing process means you don't have to apologize to anybody.
Sometimes things aren't so linear and can shift in a
matter of seconds.
But it gets easier when we can count on our greatest blessings.
We have one life and I think that's something we can be
thankful for.
There doesn't have to be an end to a life that offers
us so much more.

GAVE LOVE A SECOND CHANCE

You are the reason I gave love a second chance.
With you I have no fear when it comes to romance.
In the beginning I couldn't eat I never felt so queasy.
But after the first date I knew loving you would be easy.
With you I never have to be someone I am not.
Before you I thought about love, I thought about it a lot.
You put me first before anything and anyone.
I guess it's true what they say when you've finally found the one.
No one else compares or even comes close.
After a long day you're the person I seek the most.
You are the best thing and I'm so lucky you are mine.
You make me the happiest; you even make me rhyme.
At a point in time love wasn't exactly my best friend.
It was like running in circles and it had no end.
But when it comes to us, I look forward to all the little things.
And as I gaze towards the future, I am looking forward
to what it brings.
I still remember how we met, you grabbed my hand
and asked me to dance.
Because of you I am forever grateful I gave love a second chance.

GONE AWAY

Before you'd gone away you left me a message.
I didn't respond because you caused my heart so much wreckage.
Now all I think about is the message you left behind.
I was so hurt and confused at the time.
I told myself I would call and swore I was okay.
I even rehearsed every line and practiced what I would say.
I am so sorry I didn't call you back.
I wasn't planning on being silent like that.
I regret it each and every day.
Now I'll never know what you had to say.
Losing you wasn't easy and it's three years today.
This pain cuts deep and it hasn't gone away.
I miss you so much and I'm sorry I didn't call.
If I could talk to you one last time, I would trade it all.
Nothing hurts more than losing a parent so early on.
I try to keep strong, but my strength is all gone.
As the sun shines on my face and as the heat warms my skin.
I will think of the good times and remember what had been.
You may have left and gone away.
But my love for you is endless, forever and a day.

RUNNING TO CATCH UP TO YOU

I've been running for a while to catch up to you.
I've been lying to myself and I know you're lying too.
We keep running because we love the chase.
We have no problem with keeping up with the pace.
You know it's chemistry when it feels magnetic.
This connection is never boring only energetic.
And you may be tough I'll admit it.
But I don't mind your exterior, not one bit.
Like gravity you have a force over me.
If my heart had a lock, you would be the one with the key.
Even though we're different, we're looking for the same thing.
Meeting you was an example of what luck can bring.
And oceans separate lands but not souls.
Let's not let distance get in the way of our goals.
Maybe one day we can finally slow it down.
Because truth is; I love having you around.

FAILED ROMANCE

What I can give you in one day would take her over a decade.
We were friends first long before a romance was made.
You love her now so effortlessly.
When you and I argued repetitively.
She can love you now the way it wasn't for me.
She saved me from a love that wasn't meant to be.
She can have the changed man I left behind.
Even though I put you there I don't mind.
We are better people because of this failed romance.
Deserving of your love, you gave her a real chance.

DOMINO EFFECT

You think you know someone until they betray you.
When they don't think about what their actions can do.
They see it as a minor slip up and don't think about it twice.
So, there you stand, frozen cold as ice.
You go in shock mode because you can't believe it's true.
You can't believe something like this can happen to you.
It's sad when they lie and disregard your feelings.
I guess loyalty to some have different meanings.
Nothing cuts deeper than feeling left out.
What used to be pure now fills your head with doubt.
When one domino falls it effects the rest.
Now reality sinks in and your relationship is put to the test.

TO THE BEST OF US

You hold on because you're afraid to let go.
And there are parts you'd rather not show.
You stay quiet because it feels too real to say out loud.
You fear critics when it's only you standing in the crowd.
You settle because everyone else does too.
You had dreams but sooner or later they outgrew you.
– To the best of us

I DIDN'T WANT TO

I didn't want to get to know you because I knew I would fall.
I knew once we started talking, I would anticipate your call.
I knew if you tried, I would fall to my knees.
Because with people these days there are no guarantees.
You came into my life like a sudden beam of light.
And these feelings came with a battle I wasn't willing to fight.
I tried to shrug you off because I knew I wasn't the only one.
And once feelings are involved it cannot be undone.
Because truth is, I wasn't scared of meeting you.
I was scared of saying goodbye to a love I never knew.

MORE TIME THE BETTER

You're so perceptive and focused into me.
You let me live a real life fantasy.
You see the dimple in my smile and the sparkle in my eye.
You make it evident and it makes me shy.
You never make me question your focus when we talk.
I get this sense of sincerity, but I've hit a roadblock.
If you only knew what this all meant to me.
You wouldn't have to question what you already feel and see.
I think the more time we have the better it will be.
I just don't want you to become a distant memory.

RAINY DAY

This rain makes me want to share my heart with you.
If all we had was right now what would you do?
The raindrops fall steady, I miss having you around.
It may as well be you that's pouring down.
This rain is a reminder that you're not here with me.
Now with every thundered sky I keep you in my memory.

NEVER SETTLE FOR LESS

I am the girl guys call when they feel lonely.
They act like they have real intentions when really, they're phony.
Love is a disease and I'm just looking for the cure.
I wish I wasn't so naive to believe all hearts are pure.
Some would say I am foolish or hopelessly romantic.
But when it comes to commitment I start to panic.
Maybe because I am so used to love not working in my favor.
And with every best thing that comes along I wish
I was a lot braver.
But I'm grown now, and I know what I want.
I know now that asking for love isn't asking for a lot.
Ladies I know we all have been here before.
Please don't settle for someone who isn't willing to give you more.

SECRET SINNER

I spew out feelings, but the good ones are hard to find.
Sometimes I refrain from speaking my mind.
In my head I am a secret sinner.
It's no surprise that my outside doesn't match my inner.
I have this rage I am ready to release.
When I'm mad there's no hope for finding peace.
I may have become this silent assassin.
I kill my thoughts before they happen.
It's an internal warfare inside my head.
I'm a secret sinner for the words not said.

PAST

I don't know what hurts more.
The ones that left or the deep-down convictions I tried to ignore.
Sometimes people walk out of your life because it's harder to stay.
And in hindsight you realize it was better that way.
So, thank you for the lessons and giving me reasons to move on.
Because truth is, you can't go back now that the
feelings are all gone.
Friendships fail and relationships don't last – but who I am now
I owe all to my past.

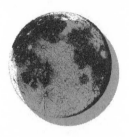

UNDER PRESSURE

Beneath the surface and under pressure.
She meets her darkness; she sees the aggressor.
Upon the weight and in the light.
She sees the truth, another delight.
What more does she have to see?
Again, she is left without an apology.
So cold she remains and heart now frozen.
Her guard goes back up as pride is chosen.
Struggling in her own headspace as she tries to be positive.
She knows it's up to her, it's her own prerogative.
Sheer proof of another fatal revelation.
And in this darkness, it led her to true liberation.

LIGHT V. DARK

It may appear as though the darkness in the sky takes up a huge
piece of territory.
But truth is the stars tell a better story.
They shine for those who are no longer living.
Despite the darkness, the light keeps on winning.

JUMPSTART MY HEART

My heart always seems to be untouchable.
I welcome many souls, but I fail to be lovable.
I allow a person to get close but far enough where I am guarded.
I allow myself to believe it's ok to be brokenhearted.
Some days are easy and some days I come tumbling down.
I go out of my way to make sure no one sticks around.
I have a case of this untouchable heart.
But maybe all my heart needs is a little jumpstart.

HEART DON'T BREAK EVEN

How can I pretend you don't mean a thing to me?
Does anyone know how to erase a memory?
Is it normal to obsess over a loss this long?
And it's been years since you've been gone.
I'm finally coming to terms with this broken heart.
Never knew it would break me apart.

SCAPEGOAT

Naturally you were impulsive and extremely insecure.
I was your scapegoat when you were feening for more.
I was the sacrifice for your narcissistic behavior.
I guess speaking my truth just wasn't your flavor.
I refused to fall victim under your tyranny.
And from your tough exterior I detected massive irony.
I was your scapegoat when things went wrong.
The reason we no longer speak is because I didn't play along.
I was a threat to you, so you smeared my name.
Then again you never played a fair game.
You were patronizing and very selfish.
Undoubtedly you had always been jealous.
But the best part about being the scapegoat
was the awakening phase.
I recognized the patterns and finally escaped your maze.

REBIRTH

Why did I ever settle for less than I deserved?
Why did I trust you when you never gave me your word?
What I have now is more than I thought love could be.
He brings out the confidence that was already inside of me.
You didn't see me drowning, gasping for air.
Just by looking at me he can tell when I am hiding my despair.
I was longing for a love that wasn't envious or mad.
Even if I am upset with him my heart is never sad.
Sometimes people serve as place holders until you
finally realize your worth.
Now our innate love feels like a sudden rebirth.

CLOSING

Everything written in this book was everything I harbored in and more. It's been well over a decade, but I am finally letting go of everything that has festered inside of me. For a while, I thought I was unlovable. I found myself in poor relationships to fill a void. I was three years old when my dad left. His absence left me thinking it was my own fault. My self-esteem plummeted and I saw myself more likely to be with men who mirrored that abandonment.

It wasn't an easy journey, but writing has become a new face of mine – a creative expression. It really helps to write down every single thought, vision and dream. I never thought my dream journal would be the source of a new inspiration and a therapeutic process. I write down my dreams as well as my pain, my abandonment and my personal struggles. Writing has offered me a positive escape and a sense of freedom that I don't feel judged for.

Please don't be so hard on yourself because things didn't work out. Unfortunately, love comes and goes, but the important thing is that you don't allow it to turn you cold. Some things are out of your control and not everyone you love leaves.

This book is sheer proof that you can turn your pain and heartbreak into something incredibly powerful. Everyone who enters our lives have something worth teaching; some lessons are painful and some are painless.

My painful lessons and losses have led me here; the start to an incredible beginning. Thank you for being a part of my journey. This means more to me than you can imagine. I hope to share more soon in the near future!

Keep the faith always,
Jamie

As long as I have these scars, I will keep on writing.

Maybe these scars aren't the only thing that can leave a mark.

Made in the USA
Middletown, DE
19 November 2020